Everything
You Need to
Know About

Misinformation on the Internet

Internet users need to develop ways of distinguishing factual content from misinformation, especially when purchasing items online or doing research.

Everything You Need to Know About

Misinformation on the Internet

Christopher D. Goranson

The Rosen Publishing Group, Inc.
New York

Published in 2002 by The Rosen Publishing Group, Inc.
29 East 21st Street, New York, NY 10010

Copyright © 2002 by The Rosen Publishing Group, Inc.

First Edition

Library of Congress Cataloging-in-Publication Data

Goranson, Christopher D.
Misinformation on the Internet / Christopher D. Goranson.
p. cm. — (The need to know library)
Includes bibliographical references and index.
ISBN 0-8239-3521-3 (lib. bdg.)
1. Computer network resources—Evaluation—Juvenile
literature. 2. Internet literacy—Juvenile literature. 3. Internet
and teenagers—Juvenile literature. 4. Internet—Safety
measures—Juvenile literature. 5. Computer crimes—
Prevention—Juvenile literature. [1. Computer network
resources—Evaluation. 2. Internet literacy. 3. Internet—
Safety measures. 4. Computer crimes—Prevention.]
I. Title. II. Series.

ZA4201 .G63 2001
004.67'8—dc21

2001003214

Manufactured in the United States of America

Contents

Introduction

It is difficult to remember a time when information was only available in printed magazines, books, or newspapers. Now, most of that material is available online along with a vast array of other data that runs the gamut from useful to useless. The Internet has changed how we view the world and how we live our lives. It has given us the power to learn, but it has also presented each user with more information than he or she could ever process. Still, it is possible to approach the Web in a constructive way.

The Internet is changing the way we think about communication. It has been a major contributing factor in both economic growth and economic slowdown. It has never been easier to create a mechanism to promote

Although the Internet can be an excellent research tool, it is also a forum for people with questionable motives.

a product, person, or idea. The Internet offers more products from which to choose, more "miracle" cures, and more information than we could ever hope to digest. Unfortunately, it has also become increasingly difficult to sort its factual information from its hype, especially for new users. It is more important than ever to know how to identify accurate and reliable facts.

Prior to the age of electronic publishing, printed material was scrutinized by many people, including editors, fact checkers, and others in the publishing industry. Today, however, with the extremely low cost of publishing on the Internet, any individual can hypothetically turn his or her ideas, products, or personal agenda into a professional-looking document within hours. It's up to the reader to learn the difference between written material that is derived from a reputable source versus that which is potentially shady. All people are now being forced to reevaluate the written word.

Still, many read with the common thought that "if it's written, it must be true." This "seeing is believing" attitude is not one that should be employed while judging information online. It is important to use critical thinking skills when deciding if a Web site has valuable, useful, and factual information. This book is a good first step to deciding how to use these skills in order to evaluate the Internet and its surge of data.

Applying trust to the Internet as a whole can be very dangerous. For one, personal agendas and other motivations aside, many voices on the Internet are only interested in gaining a visitor's trust and then using this sense of confidence to either encourage him or her to believe the statements, to make purchases, or both. In the chapters that follow we'll investigate how you can become a savvy surfer, common things to avoid, and how to separate the truth from the tricks. It is a new wild Web world.

Chapter 1

The Living Library Without an Editor

The Internet is a living library of information, changing and expanding rapidly. Web sites are almost always in the process of being reinvented, redesigned, and expanded, offering content on an even wider variety of subjects. The Web is not static; it is also not the same as turning to an ordinary public library to gather information. On the Web users can buy, sell, and auction personal items, have discussions, post messages, send e-mail, read text, and browse countless Web sites searching for even the most specific information. However, unlike the public library, the Internet's information has not been chosen by a public servant such as a librarian, who will most likely have a degree in information science. A librarian, unlike some Webmasters,

Unlike sources on the Internet, the information at public libraries has been chosen and scrutinized by a librarian trained to offer only creditable materials.

takes great care in offering only creditable materials to readers. The Internet is a new territory, often compared to a virtual marketplace, complete with stores, clubs, religious groups, government agencies, and organizations of many regions, countries, and languages. It is worldwide in its coverage of daily life, and millions of people interact with it, and each other, on a daily basis.

Just like in any city in America or anywhere else in the world, crime exists online, and the Internet can be a haven for criminals of every kind. It's important to realize that while the Internet offers a whole world of high-quality resources and information, it also opens the door to some potentially dangerous places and dangerous people.

There are many different opinions on what, if any, is an appropriate method for regulating content on the Internet. Some people think the Internet should be censored, with morally questionable or other graphic content blocked from children and minors. Others say that the Internet represents the very epitome of free speech and that any regulation, no matter how minimal, is a big mistake, as well as a violation of citizens' First Amendment rights.

Two Approaches to Internet Regulation

Under state law, a California library cannot be sued for failing to filter Internet content, according to a state appeals court decision. In the case of *Kathleen R. v. the City of Livermore*, a woman was seeking damages against the library for material that her son, aged twelve, gained access to on library computers. Regulators are trying to determine how best to block certain content with a measure known as the Children's Internet Protection Act (CIPA). But other groups oppose the new law, saying that it violates the

The First Amendment of the U.S. Constitution

The First Amendment of the U.S. Constitution, part of what is known as the Bill of Rights, helps citizens feel secure in several important freedoms, such as the freedom of religion and expression. Many people remember the First Amendment because it secures every citizen's right to freedom of speech. This law, adopted in 1791, also secures certain freedoms regarding published media, including both printed and electronic works. It states:

Congress shall make no law respecting an establishment of religion, or prohibiting the free exercise thereof; or abridging the freedom of speech, or of the press; or the right of the people peaceably to assemble, and to petition the government for a redress of grievances.

First Amendment rights protect Americans from being prohibited from simply speaking their minds, writing an article, or creating a Web page with information that they see fit, no matter its opinion or source, and offering it to the public to view.

First Amendment. A previous case in Virginia found that libraries that impose filtering could be sued under First Amendment law.

In China, the Ministry of Public Security released new software designed to keep "cults, sex, and violence" off the Internet. Called Internet Police 110, it will prevent users from gaining access to "unhealthy information from foreign and domestic Web sites," a police official was quoted as saying. China routinely blocks Web sites of Western media outlets, human rights groups, and dissident (disagreeing) groups.

Top Ten Dot-Cons

If you think you are safe on the Web, you need to think again. According to the Federal Trade Commission, the following is a list of the most frequent complaints from Internet users:

- ◎ Internet auction fraud—Consumers think they're getting a bargain, but often, what they really get is a substitute product, a portion of what they ordered, or sometimes nothing at all.

- ◎ Internet service provider scams— Consumers are told they'll get free money by simply cashing a check. But what they don't realize is that by cashing that check they've actually agreed to conditions that they didn't read in the fine print, see on the back of the check, or notice hidden in the envelope. Consumers say they've been "trapped" into long-term contracts for Internet access or another Web service, with big penalties for cancellation or early termination.

◎ Internet Web site design promotions/"Web cramming"—Customers are promised a free, custom-designed Web site for a thirty-day trial period, with no obligation to continue. But after signing the contract, they are charged on their telephone bill or receive a separate invoice—even if they never accepted the offer or discontinued the service after the thirty-day period.

◎ Internet information and adult services/ "credit card cramming"—Users are told that age verification is required to access adult images, and age verification can only be proven by providing a valid credit card number. Customers are then charged for purchases they never made on their account after providing the information.

◉ Multilevel marketing /"pyramid scams"—Customers are told they can make money through selling various products and services, and by recruiting people to do the same. When the products or services are actually sold to the customer, there is no way to make money from the program because it is then owed to the company, or the customers are actually other distributors, not the general public.

◉ Business opportunities and work-at-home scams—Often promising a very high rate of return, these business opportunities turn out to be nothing short of a scam with the numbers and earnings claims completely falsified.

◉ Investment schemes and get-rich-quick scams—By making an initial investment in a day-trading service, the schemes claim that the customer will make huge sums of money on a "small" initial investment. These programs are usually very risky, thus the claims of huge profits.

◉ Travel/Vacation fraud—Customers are told that they can get a luxurious vacation with many extras at a very inexpensive price. What usually ends up being delivered is very low-quality accommodations and services, or no trip at all. Yet customers are hit with hidden fees and charges that weren't well disclosed or revealed.

◎ Telephone/pay-per-call solicitation frauds (including modem dialers and videotext)— Customers are told they can gain free access to adult material by simply installing a "viewer" or "dialer" computer program. The programs actually dial an international long-distance number through the customers' own modems, accumulating huge charges on their phone bills.

◎ Health-care frauds—"Miracle" products or cures are sold to people who are often desperate for a speedy cure. Sometimes this can be especially harmful because some people will delay getting sufficient health care with the hopes that the "miracle" cures will actually work.

Want to know what you can do to avoid these scams? See how many solutions you can come up with on your own, then compare your list with the list at the end of chapter 5.

Chapter 2

Chat Rooms, Newsgroups, and E-Mail— How Can You Stay Safe?

"Our biggest mistake is believing the Web is innocuous. Chat room visitors should be screened no less carefully than visitors that come into your home."

—Mark Brasche, Owner, SurfSafely.com

No matter where you are on the Internet, you'll undoubtedly run into a number of other users. Most, like you, are interested in exploring information about popular subjects such as current events, movies, sports, or celebrity lifestyles, just to name a few. E-mail allows us to communicate with others; newsgroups (electronic bulletin boards) permit us to send or post messages in response to others on a wide variety of similarly grouped topics; and chat rooms allow us to interact in real time with other users. Some chat rooms now have voice support, allowing users to actually "chat" rather than simply type.

Nick was bored and decided to spend a little time online. An avid hockey fan, he found a chat room dedicated to fans of his favorite hockey team, the Colorado Avalanche. After spending an hour there, he was contacted several times by a person also claiming to be an Avalanche fan who seemed to have similar interests. He also claimed to have gone to the same school. After Nick ignored him for a while, he became more aggressive. He began asking Nick where he lived and other personal questions. Nick didn't think anything about it until he realized that his user profile had listed his home address, favorite Web sites, and where he went to school. Nick quickly removed this information to protect his privacy and safety.

One of the most popular places for Internet users to explore is a chat room. People from all around the world get together to discuss a wide range of topics—subject matter from recipes and religion to dating and divorce. Chat rooms are more interactive than most Internet experiences because users can talk with each other directly, either by typing to each other or, in some cases, speaking into a microphone and viewing the words on a computer screen at the same time. Usually, this action is referred to as a virtual experience in "real time." Unlike the standard Web site where visitors are served

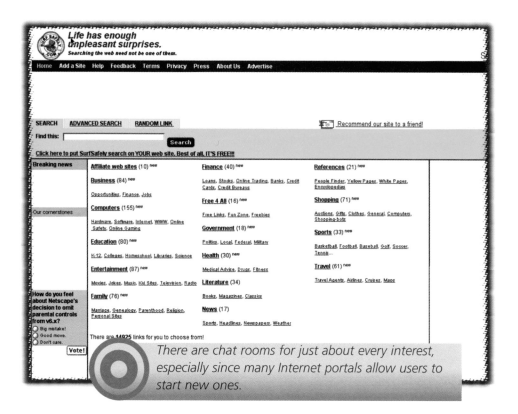

There are chat rooms for just about every interest, especially since many Internet portals allow users to start new ones.

a page of organized information, users can interact and exchange ideas, thoughts, and opinions with each other and anyone else who happens to be in the virtual room. It's sort of like the difference between reading a magazine and talking with several people on the telephone. One action doesn't replace the other (people who talk on the phone still like to read magazines), but the chat room experience offers unique options to the Web surfer that just can't be found on a Web site.

The Internet is full of ways for users to interact on many different levels. Before the more recognizable Web chat rooms came along, there was Internet relay chat, or IRC. Internet relay chat allowed users to talk with a number of other users in a variety of virtual rooms, generally based on certain types of subject matter. Some of these rooms, or channels, were very well monitored; others were monitored very little or not at all. Bulletin boards, one of the first methods of communicating with other Internet users, are essentially what they were. Bulletin boards, or message boards, are simply places where users post messages and replies to other messages that anyone may view.

Chat rooms have since graduated from the IRC format to become components that are directly placed into Web sites themselves. Any number of sites on the Internet offer a variety of chat rooms on an even broader variety of subjects. Some offer chat rooms to help build a user community, while others focus specifically on providing the chat feature. Regardless of how it is used, the chat room is an extremely popular feature of the Internet and used by a varied group of people.

However, chat rooms aren't secured areas. They can entertain and lead to the exchange of good dialogue or unique ideas, but the very nature of how and why chat rooms are popular can also make them dangerous. Depending on what chat room a user visits, there are a number of different procedures he or she must take before entering. Sometimes it's simply entering a user name, or an alias. Other times it's entering detailed information about himself or herself, like his or her real name, address, and telephone number.

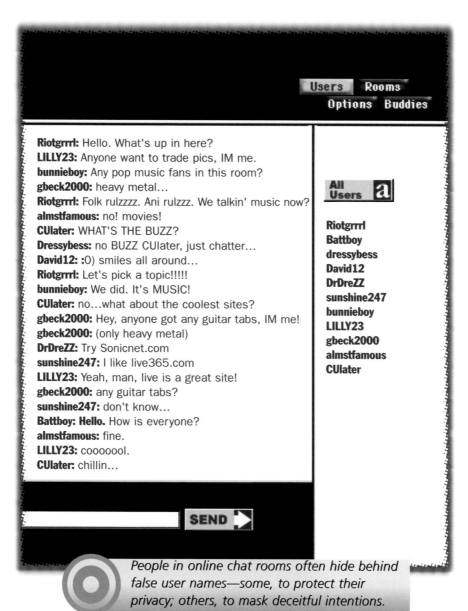

Riotgrrrl: Hello. What's up in here?
LILLY23: Anyone want to trade pics, IM me.
bunnieboy: Any pop music fans in this room?
gbeck2000: heavy metal...
Riotgrrrl: Folk rulzzzz. Ani rulzzz. We talkin' music now?
almstfamous: no! movies!
CUlater: WHAT'S THE BUZZ?
Dressybess: no BUZZ CUlater, just chatter...
David12: :0) smiles all around...
Riotgrrrl: Let's pick a topic!!!!!
bunnieboy: We did. It's MUSIC!
CUlater: no...what about the coolest sites?
gbeck2000: Hey, anyone got any guitar tabs, IM me!
gbeck2000: (only heavy metal)
DrDreZZ: Try Sonicnet.com
sunshine247: I like live365.com
LILLY23: Yeah, man, live is a great site!
gbeck2000: any guitar tabs?
sunshine247: don't know...
Battboy: Hello. How is everyone?
almstfamous: fine.
LILLY23: cooooool.
CUlater: chillin...

Users Rooms
Options Buddies

All Users

Riotgrrrl
Battboy
dressybess
David12
DrDreZZ
sunshine247
bunnieboy
LILLY23
gbeck2000
almstfamous
CUlater

SEND

People in online chat rooms often hide behind false user names—some, to protect their privacy; others, to mask deceitful intentions.

Perhaps one reason behind registering users who visit chat rooms, an action that demands that they reveal personal information, is to help filter out those users who would not be willing to supply accurate facts. Another reason could be that supplying this information could help the facilitator of the chat room verify the user's identity. Whatever the case, there is seldom any good reason for providing personal information to anyone unless you know exactly what it will be used for and who will have access to it. Many Web sites offer a privacy policy as a part of their site that outlines how personal information will be used and if it will be given to any third party.

What is the real danger of providing personal information in a chat room? Well, first of all, it's not just the service that may have access to it. In many chat rooms, a user merely has to click on your user name to find out more information about you. If you've provided factual information, this user suddenly has access to whatever personal details you've provided. The user may then use this information to manipulate you into trusting him or her. He or she may ask other personal questions that you may be uncomfortable answering. While the likelihood of someone purposefully using your personal information to try and figure out more about you may seem extreme, it really isn't. Even if he or she means you no harm, would you ever provide that information to a stranger over the telephone if he or she asked you to? Chances are you wouldn't, so why do it online?

The reality surrounding chat rooms is that you shouldn't offer information to anyone if you don't want it shared with the rest of the world. Think of it in this

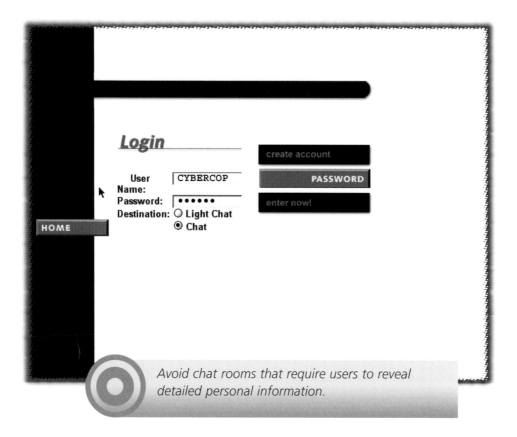

Avoid chat rooms that require users to reveal detailed personal information.

way: If you're not required to provide truthful and accurate information about yourself, can you really trust that anyone else in the chat room is really who they say they are? Law enforcement agencies have set up stings in chat rooms to help find potential criminals who prey on teens and young children. These criminals often masquerade as young adults or children themselves, trying to coerce other visitors in the chat room to offer detailed information. This is predatory behavior. As a chat room visitor, you should always remember that any personal information that you provide might endanger you. That same rule also applies to e-mail, e-commerce (buying and selling goods online), and instant messaging.

Hoaxes, Rumors, Urban Legends, and Spam

An e-mail hoax is referred to as spam, something that anyone who uses an e-mail account on a regular basis has seen, whether they are aware of it or not. Usually people think of spam as e-mail that attempts to sell you something, but spam also takes a more basic definition when referring to any unsolicited e-mail. Included in this more general understanding of spam is the ever-present e-mail hoax. An e-mail hoax often becomes a scam when the reader is asked to either send money, identify his or her password and login information, or perform an action that will benefit the sender of the e-mail, such as calling a long-distance telephone number that results in expensive charges to the recipient. In almost every case the recipient is asked to send the e-mail hoax to family and friends.

There are a number of e-mail hoaxes. This is a message that is sent to a user, or group of users, that contains false information. Commonly, these e-mail messages ask that the recipient either help an individual, group, or country, or claim to be privileged "insider" information on a stock trade, virus outbreak, recent news story, or other information. There are hundreds, sometimes thousands, of these messages circulating the Web. On any given day, for example, an average Internet user will receive several: one claiming to need assistance to search for a missing child, another delivering a false petition to "sign" and send on to as many addresses as possible, and still another that is a deceptive promotional giveaway. Ironically, these messages may seem legitimate. But there are signs that you can look for in the message or subject heading that offer clues that they are really just spam.

Most of these clues are apparent if you search for certain phrases such as, "Forward this message to everyone you know," "This is not a hoax," or any emphatic phrasing that suggests that you should forward the warning to "Protect friends and family." Additionally, be wary of any message that was forwarded a number of times. These common examples of "chain" e-mail are almost always false.

Other spam promises to make the user money through a tracking device, or is a letter or other type of message that attempts to persuade or even threaten him or her into sending the same e-mail message to others.

The e-mail hoax is generally innocuous and more annoying than harmful. However, it is considered a virus in the way that it disrupts the progress of the computer user and provides him or her with false information. It also spreads this misinformation in a similar fashion as a computer virus would.

The premise of spam is simple, yet effective. In many cases the messages allow users to believe they are getting something for nothing. There's no real point to this e-mail, other than to encourage unknowing users into demanding money or free goods and services. Yet it's an extremely effective "you've got nothing to lose and everything to gain" approach to coercing people into falling for a scheme.

Other spam carries the endorsement of familiar store names, brand names, or even celebrity names. These rumors are often scandalous messages that are sent for a joke. Others are merely urban legends such as the recent hoax that was circulating in some states about cyanide-coated mailing envelopes.

Many of these hoaxes have little clues that the discriminating user will immediately recognize. Some seem to be a game, to see how many people will fall for the hoax, or how many will understand its slight discrepancies and know that it's a hoax. E-mail hoaxes and scams use a number of clever techniques to try to convince the recipient. They may claim to be from a reliable source, such as a well-known software company or Internet service provider, a person the reader is likely to be familiar with such as a celebrity or political figure, or an organization. These e-mails will often cite reliable sources as references such as the *Wall Street*

Journal, the *New York Times*, *Business Week*, or others. However, you'll probably never see a date, page number, or link to the actual article where the original information was gathered. When verifying questionable sources, always remember that you have to verify the *entire* source. It pays to do your homework.

Scammers and cheats bet that most people are trusting and don't have time to research sources. For scammers, it's okay if only a fraction of their audience reads the e-mail and falls for the ploy. Remember, if the e-mail purports to provide the reader with something that sounds too good to be true, it probably is.

If you need help determining if e-mail messages are really legitimate, you can call the Bureau of Consumer Protection at (877) FTC-HELP (382-4357). Or, call the Mail Fraud Complaints Center of the U.S. Postal Service at (800) 372-8347.

Other Types of Fraud

Mark Simeon Jakob was a trader who had ideas about how to make a profit in the stock market by using the Internet. Jakob, aged twenty-three, had an idea to boost his return on a certain company's stock. That company was Emulex, a maker of high-speed storage products. Jakob e-mailed a false news release to Internet Wire, a company at which he had previously worked. The news release stated that Emulex was restating prior profits

FBI agents escort Mark Simeon Jakob, the man behind the Emulex hoax, from FBI headquarters in Los Angeles on August 31, 2000.

and losses, was under investigation by the Securities Exchange Commission, and its chief executive had quit. The news release was subsequently picked up by a number of other news agencies that continued to spread the false information. In a matter of minutes, stock investors panicked and dumped shares. As a result, Emulex stock dropped 62 percent while Jakob pocketed more than $241,000 in profits. (He traded shares during the wild swings of the stock's highs and lows.) The stock quickly stabilized, but the damage to both the company and to its investors had already been done. The hoax cost traders $110 million.

Jakob eventually pled guilty to two counts of securities fraud and one count of wire fraud, and faces up to forty-six months in prison. He agreed to pay $110 million in restitution, and turned over $54,000 in cash, which authorities said were proceeds from the Internet news-release hoax.

Chapter 3

The Web Isn't Foolproof—How Can You Check Its Facts?

David's English teacher has assigned his class the task of writing a research paper, a minimum of ten pages, typed, and well researched, and with cited footnotes. She also mentioned how young people are often lulled into using the Internet as their only researching tool. Because of this she asked that each student use a variety of sources, both printed and electronic. But David wondered how difficult it would be to document his electronic sources, and if they were even reliable. His topic was specific enough—photosynthesis—but he knew that if he went to his favorite search engine it would return thousands of Web pages, many of them useless. He wondered if he should bother using the Internet at all.

Because the Internet is a seamless stream of endless information, available any time of the day or night to any person, the Web is also a danger zone. It is an open invitation to a wealth of data—both factual and false. Like most people, students can find information about nearly any topic, but it is important to evaluate those so-called facts every time you seek them, especially when conducting research, checking sources, or making purchases.

A trap that many students are likely to fall into, however, is when they rely upon the Internet as their sole source of information for any purpose, whether answering a simple question for a homework assignment, or searching for additional facts for a research paper.

The Internet is an easy and attractive forum for people who have hidden agendas, want to offer subjective and persuasive writing to gain or hold your attention, or mislead you into believing something that is completely false. Students can be easily swayed into believing anything that is published on its electronic pages. Occasionally, false information is specifically targeted to young people on purpose! How can you avoid these traps? There are ways in which you can verify electronic sources, and specific guidelines that you should follow every time that you use the Internet for any purpose, even for entertainment. That is not to say that you should avoid using the Internet for the purposes of research or for help with school assignments,

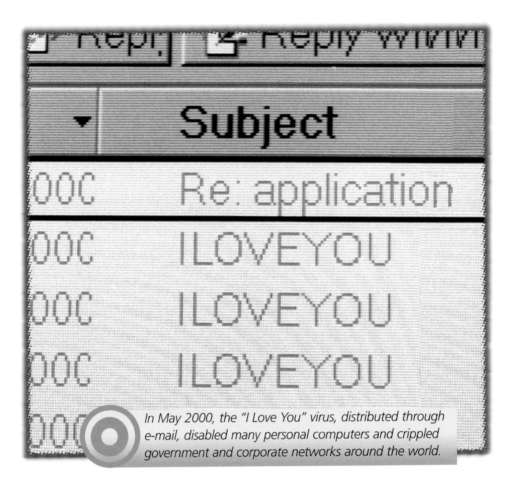

In May 2000, the "I Love You" virus, distributed through e-mail, disabled many personal computers and crippled government and corporate networks around the world.

but consider some of these points when evaluating the informational Web pages that you find online.

Learn to Be an Internet Detective

Who wrote the Web page? Does the author list his or her name and credentials, if any? Is this author the originator of this information? If not, does he or she provide a list of sources, such as links to professional organizations, universities, or other published works? Do the sources contain snail mail addresses and phone numbers that may be verified? Does the author give any other information about him or herself such as his or her occupation, affiliation, education, or related experience? Ask yourself what makes him or her an authority on the subject in question.

What is the purpose of the Web page? Do any professional organizations (schools, nonprofits, companies, and institutions) support the information on the page by supplying the site? Does the author's connection with that institution influence his or her opinion about the subject? Is the site bombarded with flashy advertisements? If so, are they connected in any way with the information that it is offering?

What is the quality of the information? When was the Web site updated? Does it appear to be updated regularly? How does the information compare to other similar facts found in books on the same subject? What seems to be the site's general purpose? Is the information derived from a printed source such as a book or magazine? Is the tone of the writing one which intends only to inform and not persuade? Does the site have multiple "outlinks" (destination sites related to its topic) that are creditable and current, or "blind links" that cannot be found? Does the site appear to have good grammar and accurate spelling? Is the site finished, or is it "under construction?"

Who is the intended audience for the Web page? Many times, the Web offers "rings" of sites that are linked together by like-minded individuals who share an interest in a certain topic. While they may seem to provide complete or accurate information, these connected sites are often forums for people who share a common interest or enthusiasm for the subject on which the sites are focused. In most cases they cannot be relied upon as good sources for any type of research and are merely thought of as entertainment.

These are just some of the questions that you can ask yourself while you're evaluating a specific Web site. Other good suggestions are to begin your search from a notable search engine or with institutional Web sites that provide creditable links to similar places of interest. For example, it you wanted information about Lyme disease, you might begin your search at the Centers for Disease Control (CDC) Web site (http://www.cdc.gov). This government site, which provides its own internal search engine, as do many organizational sites, offers the user more than 1,000 documents about Lyme disease that are endorsed, so to speak, by the CDC. By searching in this way, instead of just punching in the words "Lyme disease" in the search engine provided by your personal Internet portal page, you are almost guaranteed a variety of creditable sites to begin your research. While it might take a moment to think of a good starting site, it's worth a great deal when you consider how much misleading information you can eliminate simply by beginning with a reliable source.

A Word About Contests

Web sites, like businesses, come in all shapes and sizes, and sometimes the sites you have to watch out for are the ones you would least suspect. Many Web sites that seem to be legitimate sources of valuable information for writers or gateways that may lead to a future in the publishing industry are really only an online forum for making a profit. Many of these sites offer a number of contests available to amateur writers. Most are, in fact, legitimate. They contain a number of resources for aspiring authors such as links to other sites that offer reference materials or teach various techniques.

Although entry into most contests is free, writers are asked for payments if their material is selected, and occasionally, as sections of a physically bound book. But that's the hook. Yes, entry into the contests is free. Yes, if you are selected as a finalist, your writing will be published.

Critics have pointed out that there seems to be little if any review of the material submitted. It seems that

NATIONAL FRAUD INFORMATION CENTER

National Fraud Information Center

1-800-876-7060

 WHAT TO REPORT

- The NFIC accepts reports about attempts to defraud consumers on the telephone or the Internet.
- Telemarketing fraud can involve companies calling consumers or consumers calling companies in response to a mailing or other form of advertising. It also includes telephone sales pitches to businesses.
- Internet fraud can include promotions found on websites, in chat rooms, newsgroups and bulletin boards, as well as via email.
- The NFIC does <u>not</u> accept reports about home improvement, auto sales, or other transactions that usually take place at consumers' homes or retail stores.

 HOW TO REPORT

- The best way to report possible fraud to the NFIC is by calling our toll-free number, **1-800-876-7060**, so that our counselors can ask for the information we need.

- Another way to make a report is to use our

- If you wish to
- If you want to

Report sites that you suspect to be scammers to agencies and other organizations that track fraud on the Internet.

anyone who submits writing for review gets accepted, no matter the quality of that writing. But this is what is known as vanity publishing. The only difference here is that this type of vanity publishing or what others may call joint-venture, subsidy, or shared responsibility publishing, is that it occurs online, and potentially, in print. This type of publishing—whether online or in print— preys on people's desires to see their work published. It's unlikely you'll ever see one of these books in a bookstore because their content is of lesser quality than books that are subjected to rigid editorial standards.

The point is that even though a Web site looks legitimate and appears to have factual content, it may not make the site legitimate. Internet users should always research a site and understand what they're buying before making a purchase. Using a credit card can often offer an added level of security, especially if the products you've ordered never arrive, are damaged, or are incorrect.

When a Dot-Org Really Isn't a Dot-Org

Everyone's heard of dot-com, dot-net, dot-org, and the rest, but what do those extensions mean? Usually, when someone thinks of a dot-com, they think of a high profile, commercial Internet site. This tends to make sense, as the dot-com stands for "commercial." But what is a dot-org? Often used by nonprofit organizations, groups, or charities, people tend to think of a dot-org as a validation for a particular Web site. For example, only appropriate government sites may obtain a dot-gov extension, and only certain higher education institutions may obtain a dot-edu. For many, it would seem a natural conclusion that a dot-org extension signifies some type of specific status, or a validation of a certain organization, but that's not the case. The truth is that anyone can apply for a dot-org just as easily as they may for a dot-com. The extension dot-com, dot-net, and dot-org are only limited by their availability.

It's important for consumers to realize that just because a dot-org is called a dot-org doesn't make it any type of official organization. Using such an extension can be a ploy used by scammers to help convince unwary surfers that what they are reading is valid. As with anything on the Internet, it never hurts to verify references or to ask the Webmaster of the site for them, especially if you're considering making a purchase from or donation to that site.

Chapter 4

It's All About the Money

The Internet is full of Web sites and "businesses" claiming to be something they're not. Mixed with all of the brand names on the Internet such as Amazon, eBay, and Yahoo!, there are thousands of other, smaller sites masquerading as secondary versions of the most popular ones on the Web. Some are completely legitimate. Others are hoping to feed off of any visitor scraps from the larger e-commerce giants. Still others appear to be e-commerce giants themselves, but may actually be nothing more than a virtual "front."

When shopping, people normally take several factors into consideration, such as price, quality, variety, appearance, satisfaction, and accessibility. The Internet drastically changes all of these factors. Most e-commerce sites handle these characteristics differently and have changed the typical dynamic of customer and business interaction.

- ◎ Location. Location on the Internet means nothing. For instance, a well-known e-commerce site could have spent millions of dollars on advertising and product development, while a newer Web site with a very similar name could also benefit from the same expensive advertising and promotion. The second, less-recognized Web site might act very differently in that its products may be of lesser quality, its services poor, and its policies shady. For the average surfer, however, a respected name is synonymous with a respected brand, and confusing the customer is exactly the goal that the lesser-known Web site wants to achieve.

- ◎ Inventory. Unlike the Internet, a retail store gives shoppers an immediate sense of how much business it does, as well as the selection of its available goods. On one hand, if you walk down the aisle of your local grocery store and the shelves are empty, you can easily deduct that the store isn't well-stocked. On the other hand, if you are visiting an e-commerce site, it may appear that it has access to a wide variety of products based on the images used on that site. In reality, the Web business may have little or no inventory. Once you've placed the order, you have no option but to wait an undetermined amount of time to receive your goods.

◉ Quality and price. A product's quality is always easier to measure when you have it in hand. Pictures don't always tell the truth, especially when you're looking at a small digital image and have nothing to compare it to. Its price may also be deceiving. The price of any item that you find online might seem inexpensive, but consider the amount of money you might have to add to your total cost for shipping and handling.

◉ Store appearance. Comparing one physical store to another is fairly straightforward in the real world. On the Internet, however, shoppers should adopt more of a "buyer beware" mentality. An attractive storefront is much easier to create online than in a retail store.

◎ Customer service. The appearance of any
Web site can be very deceiving. Do your
homework. If something sounds too good
to be true, chances are it is, regardless of
how the Web site is designed. Web sites
are also very portable. For instance, there
isn't much stopping an e-commerce site
that processed your credit card for a $400
order yesterday from disappearing tomor-
row. Or, as they did in the late 1990s and
early 2000, simply declaring bankruptcy
and leaving you footing the bill.

The National Fraud Information Center's Five Things to Look for When Shopping Online

1. *Look for a privacy policy.* Reputable
   Web sites will tell you how your information will be used and by whom. Look
   for policies that allow users to determine
   whether or not personal information is
   accessible to third parties.

2. *Gather information about the offer.*
   Companies should provide information

about the service or product they are selling, including information about guarantees, warranties, return or cancellation policies, and whom to contact if customers have any questions.

3. *Gather information about the seller.* Every site should contain a physical address and telephone number for the seller. If a problem occurs, customers should have the ability to contact the seller easily.

4. *Obtain a date of delivery.* Find out when you will receive the product or when the services will be performed. Make a record of your transaction in an e-mail message.

5. *Ask about the Web site's security.* Find out how the Web site protects your information when it is transmitted and stored. Look for an indication on your browser that you are, in fact, making the transaction over a secure server. You should see an unbroken key or closed lock icon indicating that you are on a secure server. Remember never to send valuable information such as credit card numbers through e-mail.

Keeping Personal Information Private

Your private information is called private for a reason—it's yours to give out to whomever you choose, or to keep away from whomever you want. There is great power in your personal information, and many people want that power. In your hands, it identifies you; in the hands of someone else, your private information can actually become a weapon to be used against you. Companies commonly use this type of information for marketing and can sell it to other companies to do the same thing. The result is a seemingly unending string of unsolicited calls, junk mail, and e-mail. Keep in mind that your information can be sold again ten times or more to businesses that will call you, send you junk mail, and try to get something out of you.

Sometimes, it's difficult to remember to deliberately avoid situations that ask you to reveal personal information. In fact, in the very early days of the Internet, it was a common practice for many businesses to intentionally survey young people, luring them to answer personal questions about themselves and their family in exchange for a promotional gift. Luckily, in 1998, Congress passed the Children's Online Privacy Protection Act (COPPA) in order to stop this collection of data by commercial Web sites who specifically targeted young people. After COPPA was passed, Web businesses could not gain any type of information from children under the age of thirteen without parental consent.

Still, there are additional ways in which each person can help protect his or her own private information. One step that you can take is to clear your computer's cache file after you browse the Web. This file, which is accessible through your computer's hard drive, saves a copy of every Web page that you've visited, both its text and its images. Most computers will allow this purge of information simply by going to your preferences folder and clicking on the "Empty Cache" button. Always consult your computer manual or call technical support if you have any questions about deleting files on your hard drive.

Understanding Cookies

Cookies are bits of information that your computer automatically collects without your knowledge. This information is then stored on your hard drive. It could include data about specific Web sites you visit and which operating systems and browser software you use. Using cookies has become a popular way for tracking an Internet user's habits. The use of cookies has alarmed privacy activists because it is seen as a personal invasion into private information. Many people believe that the information collected by cookies could be made available to marketers to help profile individual users.

Cookies are employed every time you surf the Web. For instance, when your Web browser sends a request to a server (the computer that hosts a Web site that your browser downloads), the server responds with specific material. The cookie or specific computer code is embedded within the documents flowing back and forth on the Web. Cookies could be used to customize information for users, sending related material based on Web sites they have already visited. Some newer versions of popular Internet software, such as Netscape Navigator and Internet Explorer, allow users to block the use of cookies or tell users when cookies are being transferred. Recent developed privacy preferences allow users to delete the use of cookies, too, simply by searching for files named "cookies.txt" or "MagicCookie" and then deleting them.

Fortunately, the use of cookies is now being monitored by the Internet Engineering Task Force (IETF), a watchdog group of international citizens who share a concern for the development and evolution of the Internet. Although the group is open to all interested individuals, it is largely operated by network designers, operators, vendors, and researchers who are all very familiar with the functionality of computer networks. One of the main tasks of the IETF is to develop new guidelines for the appropriate use of cookies. They are hoping that their findings help software developers and programmers design new software that will allow users to actively participate in the collection of cookie data. In this way, users could offer their consent before any data is collected, and also create simple, effective ways to delete this collected information from their hard drives.

Internet Checks and Balances

There are also a number of online services that provide a way for you to do some Web site investigating before you buy.

◉ www.epinions.com—Epinions.com is a site that allows users of various products and services to rate them on a competitive scale. You can find information on many e-tailers.

◉ www.gomez.com—Gomez.com issues a "report card" on a number of e-tailers, covering everything from electronics to car rental agencies. You can examine specific criteria for each Web site and see exactly where a particular business scored well, or poorly, and why.

◉ www.bizrate.com—Bizrate.com also ranks sites based on their overall performance in a number of different categories. It scans the current prices for a particular product in various e-commerce stores and returns that price range to visitors via e-mail along with the ranking of each of the respective e-tailors.

Chapter 5

Be an Internet Sleuth

"[Parents and teens should] take the journey together.
— Mark Brasche, Owner, SurfSafely.com

If you keep a lighthearted approach to recognizing the evil underpinnings of the Internet, you may be more prone to identifying those less-than-legitimate Web sites that are lurking in its shadows. By becoming an Internet sleuth you'll open your mind to spotting the tricks and tactics of those illicit sites. Every Web surfer should also maintain a steady awareness when keeping his or her online privacy, whatever the situation.

Keeping a handle on that personal information may become easier in the future. It's extremely tempting for companies to offer your information to others, even after they may have implied or agreed that they won't. In response to this fact, a new bill called the Spyware

Control and Privacy Protection Act of 2001, introduced by Senator John Edwards, hopes to protect consumers from user-installed software that collects data anonymously. This information, secretly extracted by internal computer software, is then transmitted over the Internet to the vendor. The collected facts are typically that of the user's habits and a record of which sites he or she visits. Some of the larger software companies are employing such information-collecting practices. Several lawmakers are taking a progressive stance toward curbing the amount of information a company can make available without abiding by certain policies and alerting customers to changes in their privacy policy.

The Road to Becoming a Savvy Internet User

Practical experience can be one of the best ways to learn how to play it safe on the Net. And, as suggested by SurfSafely.com, taking the journey down the information superhighway with a parent can be a very eye-opening experience. It's important for parents to fully understand the Internet and to take some time to explore it with their children. After spending just a few hours a week doing this, the exact quantity of available information, both good and bad, will become readily apparent. The ease of access to exorbitant amounts of quality information will also become obvious.

SurfSafely.com

Surfsafely.com is a different kind of search engine. A Web site that relies on Webmasters who rate their own content, SurfSafely.com provides parents and teens with a way to search the Net without any surprises. Meta tags are used by Webmasters to identify a page's content for "robots" or "spiders" that patrol the Internet for new content. The tags are hidden in the page's code and help the search engines categorize a Web site. Meta tags are similar to a card catalog in a library because they store information about a specific title and allow you to search based on a subject, title, or author name.

The owner of SurfSafely.com, Mark Brasche, created the search engine after his thirteen-year-old daughter received an unsolicited e-mail message with a direct hyperlink to a pornographic Web site. Since then, Brasche has been working diligently to create a site that provides self-regulated content without surprises. It doesn't mean that adult-related content and discussions cannot take place, but there are no links to pornography, graphic material, or anything that wouldn't be appropriate for the entire family. Surfsafely.com indexes only PICS-rated sites. It is also a self-regulating entity and periodically checks all Web sites in its index to make sure they are compliant. The response from both children and parents has been very positive.

The purpose of SurfSafely.com is to regulate content. There are some people who strongly believe that no one person should be trying to control the Internet. However, because SurfSafely.com is a privately held Web site and is not funded by any government programs, the market for content-regulated searching really drives the site's popularity. And certainly, no one is under any obligation to use the site at all. People who do use it state that it simply fills a void in the market for those consumers who want only filtered, family-friendly content.

The popularity of SurfSafely.com seems to be growing. Most important, it seems that Webmasters are making an effort to take the extra steps to provide site-regulated content.

Is Rating the Internet a Mistake?

Many people believe that the Internet is a forum that should be kept free of any rating systems. Published materials are protected under the First Amendment, so activists argue that developing a rating system for the Internet is the first step to creating a government-regulated Web. Others feel that rating the Internet will discourage its individuality and make it a homogenized (uniform) resource dominated by commercial Web sites. There are no hard and fast answers to regulating the fastest-growing public resource ever, but

just as there are people who are demanding the need
for regulation, there are an equal number who defend
the liberated content of the Web, explaining its need
for diversity.

Protecting Yourself from the Top Ten Dot-Cons

The Federal Trade Commission makes suggestions to
help Internet users protect themselves from business-
related Internet fraud.

⦿ Internet auction fraud—When bidding in
an online Internet auction, try paying
with a credit card or using an escrow service. Both methods will offer you more
protection than paying by check or cash.
Also, most services rank the sellers
based on past performance. Make sure to
find out as much as you can about the
seller *before* you buy his or her goods.

⦿ Internet service provider scams—If you
receive a check at your home or business,
read the entire document (both the front
and back) very carefully. Look for hidden
conditions written on attached materials,
or materials loosely placed within the
envelope's contents.

◎ Internet Web site design promotions/ "Web cramming"—Inspect the offer thoroughly, and ask for references. Review your phone bills carefully, and challenge any charges that you don't recognize. Remember to act immediately.

◎ Internet information and adult services/ "credit card cramming"—Always protect your credit card information diligently, and only share your information with those companies that you trust. Dispute any unauthorized charges immediately by complaining to the bank that issued the card. Federal law limits your liability to $50 in charges if your card is misused.

◎ Multilevel marketing/"pyramid scams"— Try to avoid any plans that require you to recruit distributors, buy expensive inventory, or commit to a minimum sales volume.

◎ Business opportunities and work-at-home scams—Find others who have started or currently maintain a business through the company and find out what they think about their experiences. Get all promises from the company in writing, and review the contract thoroughly before signing.

By requesting that an attorney or accountant review the business and contract, you can secure an unbiased personal opinion and be made aware of laws or other concerns that you might have missed.

◉ Investment schemes and "get-rich-quick" scams—Research the promoter and find out its standing with state and federal securities and commodities regulators. Find out how long it has been in business and what is behind the promotion. Talk to others who have invested in the program and ask them to describe their experiences. If you know someone in that particular industry, see if he or she has ever heard of the organization or knows anything about it.

◉ Travel/Vacation fraud—Always get references on any travel company. Get all details in writing, including the cancellation policy, and any other stipulations before signing any contracts.

◉ Telephone/pay-per-call solicitation frauds (including modem dialers and videotext)— Always behave cautiously when downloading anything from the Internet. Many questionable programs are wrought with viruses or contain other content that can silently damage your computer. Carefully read all agreements prior to downloading any software. Always review your phone bill and challenge any suspicious charges immediately.

◎ Health-care frauds—Consult with your doctor or a health care professional about any "cure-all" products or remedies. Be particularly suspicious of anything passed off as a "miracle" cure or any quick and easy solutions to serious ill-nesses or disease.

In Conclusion

Take time to identify useful Web sites, but also understand the amount of misleading information that is available on the Web. The Internet is a vast library of wonderful data, but before you can do anything with its content, you must first be aware that it exists. By exploring teen- and parent-friendly portal sites, areas affiliated with creditable institutions and organizations, you'll begin to identify some excellent resources on a variety of subjects. The more informed you are, the less likely you are to become a victim of the Internet's potentially misleading information.

Glossary

browser   A program on your computer such as Netscape, that you use to view files found on the Internet, such as Web sites.

cache file   A file located in your computer's hard drive (memory) that stores information such as which Web sites you have browsed.

chat room   A virtual room, or place where two or more users interface with each other. The virtual place where a chat session is held.

cookies   Messages that are sent by a Web server to your Web browser. Your browser stores these files as text files. These messages are later sent back to the Web server and identify you to that server.

download   To retrieve a file from a remote location. For example, you might download the newest version of Internet Explorer from Microsoft's Web site. Conversely, to upload means to send a file to a remote location.

e-mail   Electronic mail sent between people, similar to real mail, or snail mail, over the Internet. However, e-mail is not secure, and because it travels between many different locations during its transmission, it can be intercepted and read.

FTP   File transfer protocol. FTP is a common way to move files between different Internet sites or between an Internet site and other Internet users.

hypertext link   A clickable portion of text or an image that allows you to jump from one page to another on the Web.

Internet relay chat (IRC)   IRC is a chat system that was developed by Jarkko Oikarinen in Finland in the late 1980s.

newsgroups   A form of bulletin board that allows Internet users to send and read messages. To access newsgroups, you need access to a news server and must have a capable news-ready reader, or browser. Many Internet service providers provide this ability; sometimes referred to as Usenet.

spam   Generally refers to junk e-mail or newsgroup postings, and is usually some sort of advertisement or solicitation. "Spam" is also a verb that means to send one e-mail message to many recipients.

virus   Malicious code that runs against the owner's wishes; many are self-replicating. Some viruses are capable of wiping out entire hard drives, others serve no purpose other than to annoy.

For More Information

Federal Trade Commission
CRC-240
Washington, DC 20580
(800) FTC-HELP (382-4357)
Web site: http://www.ftc.gov

The Internet Watch Foundation
Five Coles Lane, Oakington
Cambridgeshire CB4 5BA
United Kingdom
+44 (0) 1223 237700
e-mail: admin@iwf
Web site: http://www.iwf.org.uk/safe/index.htm

TRUSTe
1180 Coleman Avenue, Suite 202
San Jose, CA 95110
(408) 494-4950
e-mail: inquiries@truste.org
Web site: http: //www.truste.org

Web Sites

The Better Business Bureau Online
http://www.bbbonline.org

Center for Media Education
http://www.kidsprivacy.org

CyberAngels
http://www.cyberangels.org

Federal Consumer Information and Programs
http://www.consumer.gov

Federal Trade Commission's Kidz Privacy Site
http://www.ftc.gov/bcp/conline/edcams/kidzprivacy/
    index.html

GetNetWise
http://www.getnetwise.org

Internet ScamBusters
http://www.scambusters.org

National Fraud Information Center
http://www.fraud.org

Net Nanny
http://www.netnanny.com

Surf Monkey
http://www.surfmonkey.com

SurfSafely.com
http://www.surfsafely.com

WiredKids
http://www.wiredkids.org

Yahooligans!
http://www.yahooligans.com

For Further Reading

Aftab, Parry. *The Parent's Guide to Protecting Your Children in Cyberspace.* New York: McGraw-Hill, 2000.

Brasche, Mark. *Child Safety-Net: How to Protect Your Children from Harm Online.* New England Webmasters, 1999.

Croft, Jennifer. *Everything You Need to Know About Staying Safe in Cyberspace.* New York: The Rosen Publishing Group, 1999.

Gelman, Robert B., and Stanton McCandlish. *Protecting Yourself Online: The Definitive Resource on Safety, Freedom, and Privacy in Cyberspace.* New York: HarperCollins, 1998.

Gralla, Preston. *Online Kids: A Young Surfer's Guide to Cyberspace.* Rev. ed. New York: John Wiley & Sons, 1999.

Petersen, Evelyn, and Karin Petersen. *E-Parenting: Using the Internet and Computers to Be a Better Parent.* Indianapolis, IN: Sams Publishing, 2000.

Index

About the Author

Christopher D. Goranson is the founder of ROW14 Web Design House (http://www.row14.com) and is also the IT project manager for Pacific Western Technologies, Ltd. He is active in the Web design and GIS community, recently completing a term as president of the Rocky Mountain chapter of the Urban and Regional Information Systems Association. Goranson has a B.A. in economics and currently resides in Denver, Colorado, with his fiancée, Lindsay.

Acknowledgments

Many thanks to my fiancée, Lindsay, and my family for their continued support.

Photo Credits

Cover © Corbis; pp. 2, 7, 10, 28 © Index Stock; p. 32 © Wide World Photos/AP.

Design

Tom Forget

Layout

Nelson Sá